SHOW DAD HOW

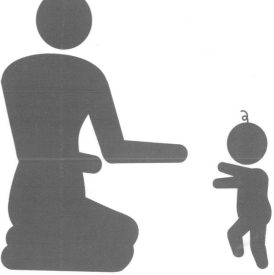

SHOW DAD

play

a note from shawn

48 deliver a baby in the subway

16 power through the market

I am a father, and that means nothing. I am a dad, and that means everything. Anyone can be a father, and anyone has for about 50,000 years (fertility is the only requirement). But being a dad requires a much higher level of perseverance, dedication, and excellence. There are musicians, and there are stars. There are soldiers, and there are warriors. There are fathers, and there are dads. Darth Vader said, "Luke, I am your father." He didn't say, "Luke, I am your dad."

To help convert more fathers to dads, I created a book specifically for us. Why? Because moms and dads come into the parenting process in completely different ways. The mother-baby connection begins long before the water breaks. Mom makes conscious diet and lifestyle decisions during the conception and gestation periods. For dad, the connection largely begins in the delivery room. In other words, when the baby is born, dad is on Day 1, and mom is on Day 462.

24 write a daddy bucket list

Because dad is on his own journey, he needs his own guidebook—but not one of those parenting tomes with hundreds of pages of tiny type.

And so **Show Dad How**, packed with easy-to-follow, step-by-step illustrations, was born. (Natural delivery, by the way. No epidural or c-section needed.)

This is the book I wish I had when my first kid was born. You no longer have to worry about what your wife can eat when she's pregnant (#16), what it takes to baby-proof a home (#30), or what to pack for the hospital (#42). But this book goes well beyond the basics. Do you know how to rig a phone as a baby monitor? We can help (#72). Wish you had a color chart for your baby's poops? We thought you'd never ask (#81). Is she going into labor on the subway? We can help with that too (#48). From mixing formula (#77) to making a daddy bucket list (#24), **Show Dad How** has you covered.

My grandfather didn't go to the hospital during my father's delivery. My father sat in the waiting room when I was born. I held my wife's leg as my sons, Jackson and Tanner, came into the world. The modern dad is still evolving, and needs information and enlightenment to keep doing so. Think of **Show Dad How** as an illustrated instruction manual for the second most important job in the history of mankind.

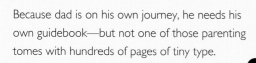

mix formula the right way 77

rig a phone as a baby monitor 72

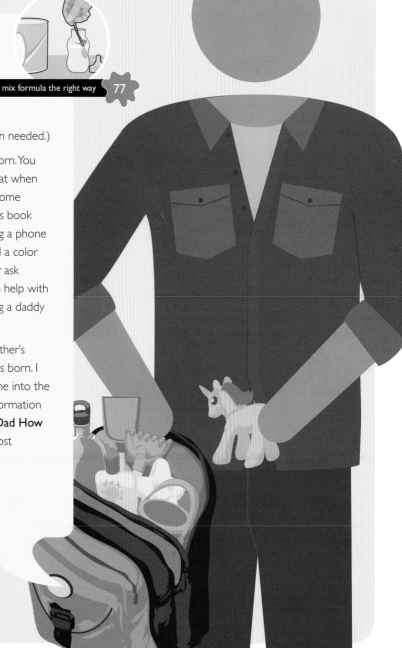

how to use this book

In the pages that follow, virtually every piece of essential information is presented graphically. In most cases the pictures do, indeed, tell the whole story. In some cases though, you'll need a little extra information to get it done right. Here's how we present those facts.

139 serve green eggs and ham

Mix eggs with food coloring. | Add greens; scramble. | Cook thoroughly. | Serve with chopped ham.

140 go on an animal cracker safari

Arrange finger foods. | Strap baby in. | Add animal crackers. | Go on safari.

snack on a pita pizza 141

Spread sauce on pitas. | Sprinkle on cheese. | Get silly with toppings. | Bake, slice, and serve.

create fun gelatin shapes 142

Mix juice and gelatin. | Heat additional juice. | Combine juices. | Stir until gelatin dissolves.

Pour into ungreased pan. | Refrigerate until set. | Cut and remove shapes. | Eat and enjoy.

ZOOMS These little circles zoom in on a step's important details, or depict the step's crucial "don'ts."

MEASUREMENTS When measurements matter, find them right in the box.

1 c
(240 ml)

3 ft
(1 m)

TOOLS Everything you'll need to perform an activity appears in the toolbars. Having a hard time deciphering an item? Turn to the tools glossary in the back of the book.

CROSS-REFERENCES When one thing just leads to another, we'll point it out. Follow the links for related or interesting information.

remove stubborn stains 90

ICON GUIDE Throughout the book, handy icons show you just how it's done. Here are the icons you'll encounter.

 Check out the timer to learn how much time a relatively short task takes.

 Repeat the depicted action the designated number of times.

 The calendar shows how many days, weeks, or months an activity requires.

 Phew—fumes! Open a window before performing this activity.

 Look to the thermometer to learn the temperature needed for a given action.

 Follow the * symbol to learn more about the how and why of the given step.

SAFETY NOTES When doing the activities in this book, always take care to ensure that you and your child are safe. Keep these guidelines in mind:

- During and after pregnancy, Mom should consult a physician before attempting any activity involving physical exertion, or whenever her condition could impair or limit her ability to engage in an activity. Stay conscious of her limits and help out with strenuous tasks.

- Do not leave your child unattended, even for a brief moment, during any activity. Be particularly cautious when participating in any activity involving water because of the risk of drowning.

- Keep small items, such as coins and candy, out of baby's reach. Any item smaller than 1¾ inches (4.5 cm), even a latex balloon or piece of paper, is a choking hazard. A good rule of thumb: if it can fit through a toilet paper roll, it is not safe for play.

- Also make sure that any string is no longer than 7 inches (18 cm). Never leave your baby unattended with ribbons or strings, as they could pose a strangulation hazard.

- Before trying an activity, assess whether it's appropriate for your child's level of development. Use writing and crafts materials that are nontoxic and have been approved for your child's age.

- See #30 for tips on making your home safer for baby; for example, remove crib mobiles once your baby can push up onto hands and knees.

A fertilized egg smaller than a pinhead will one day borrow your car keys. Hard to imagine, right? It's a journey that starts long before 300 million sperm become fierce contestants on *Survivor: Fallopian Tube*. Preparation is key. For the mom-to-be, that means seeing her doctor, taking prenatal vitamins, and tracking her monthly cycle. Luckily, the primary chore on the man's to-do list is trying to conceive, which is the most fun a guy will have in his entire life. (No, seriously.) But don't think success on that front means you're on hiatus until delivery day. A dad is born nine months before a baby is born. His job begins when the pregnancy test displays a plus sign.

prep

You love spending time
with other people's kids.

Your personal finances
are in order.

60 introduce baby to pets

You treat the pets like kids.

You have support
troops nearby.

Jean-Claude or
Arnold . . .

You're pondering
baby names.

You think pregnant
women look hot.

She's leaving hints.

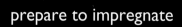

Get as healthy as possible.

Ditch any vices.

Talk it over with the doctor.

Review your prescriptions.

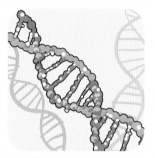

Research your genetics.

Keep cool.

Steer clear of bad influences.

Practice baby-making.

 It's good to get a full physical and discuss your plans with your doctor.

3   get in position to conceive

Up the odds of success by choosing positions that allow deep penetration and get semen closer to the cervix.

Make missionary magic.

Get behind her.

Spoon.

Stay on top.

Avoid standing positions.

4   try for a boy

Male sperm swim faster and die more quickly than female sperm. So if you want a boy, adjust your lovemaking routine to get those speedy Y chromosomes to a ready egg stat!

Offer her some potassium.

Have coffee before sex.

Use rear entry.

Have sex after ovulation.

5   try for a girl

Sperm carrying the X chromosome travel more slowly to the egg and stay frisky longer than Y-carrying sperm. If you want a girl, use conception conditions that favor these slow and steady sperm.

Suggest magnesium to her.

Take a warm bath first.

Make it missionary style.

Have sex before ovulation.

So just how are babies made? Once a month, during ovulation, an egg is released from a woman's ovary. If the egg is fertilized on its way to the uterus, it will implant and grow. If not, it will be shed along with the uterine lining.

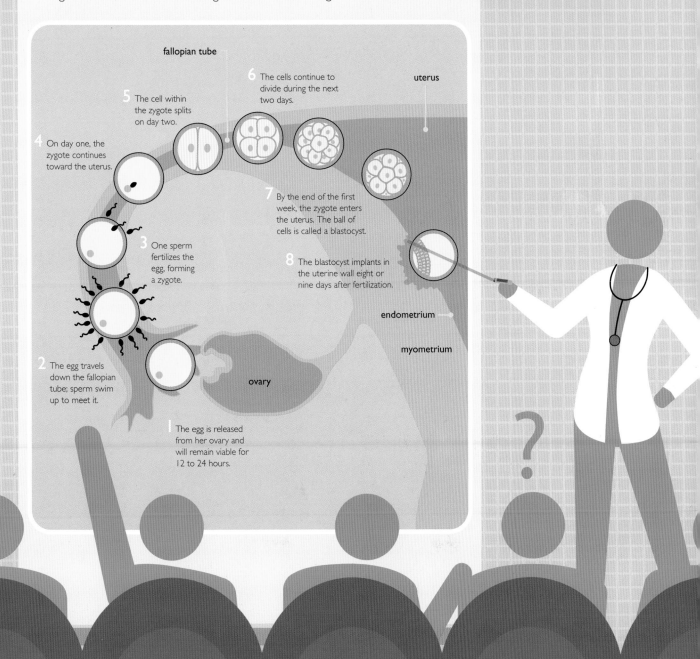

fallopian tube

6 The cells continue to divide during the next two days.

uterus

5 The cell within the zygote splits on day two.

4 On day one, the zygote continues toward the uterus.

7 By the end of the first week, the zygote enters the uterus. The ball of cells is called a blastocyst.

3 One sperm fertilizes the egg, forming a zygote.

8 The blastocyst implants in the uterine wall eight or nine days after fertilization.

endometrium

myometrium

2 The egg travels down the fallopian tube; sperm swim up to meet it.

ovary

1 The egg is released from her ovary and will remain viable for 12 to 24 hours.

She may not know she's pregnant yet, but her body is sending her clues. The following signs may be hints that there's a baby in your future.

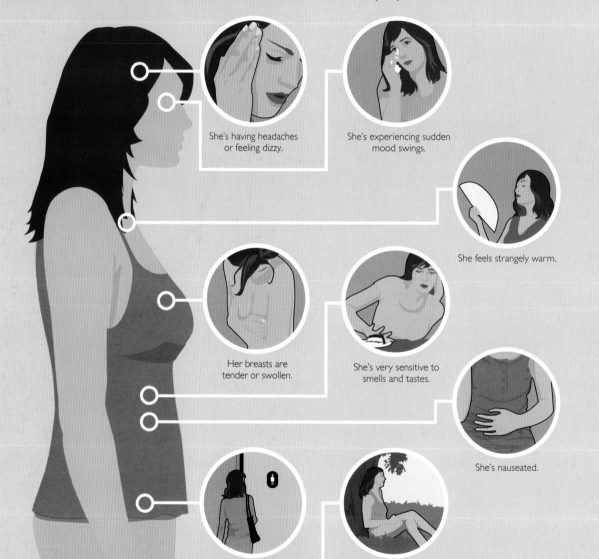

She's having headaches or feeling dizzy.

She's experiencing sudden mood swings.

She feels strangely warm.

Her breasts are tender or swollen.

She's very sensitive to smells and tastes.

She's nauseated.

She needs to pee frequently.

She is compelled to sit down or nap at odd times.

When you get the good news, use these tips to handle the moment with style and class.

Take a deep breath.

Embrace her.

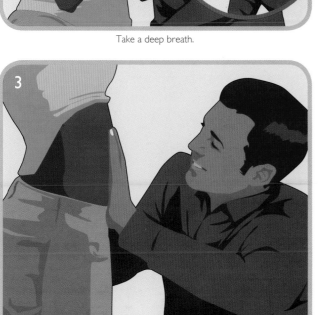

Introduce yourself.

Celebrate together.

Do you feel pregnant too? Sympathy pains are not uncommon. Couvade syndrome is a condition where an expecting father experiences the symptoms of pregnancy along with mom.

Watch out for sudden mood swings.

Be prepared to face some sleepless nights.

Look out for morning sickness.

107 get fit anywhere

Gird yourself for extra girth.

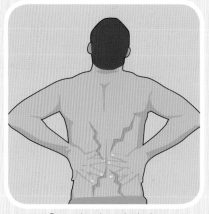

Get ready to brave backaches.

Brace yourself for anxious moments.

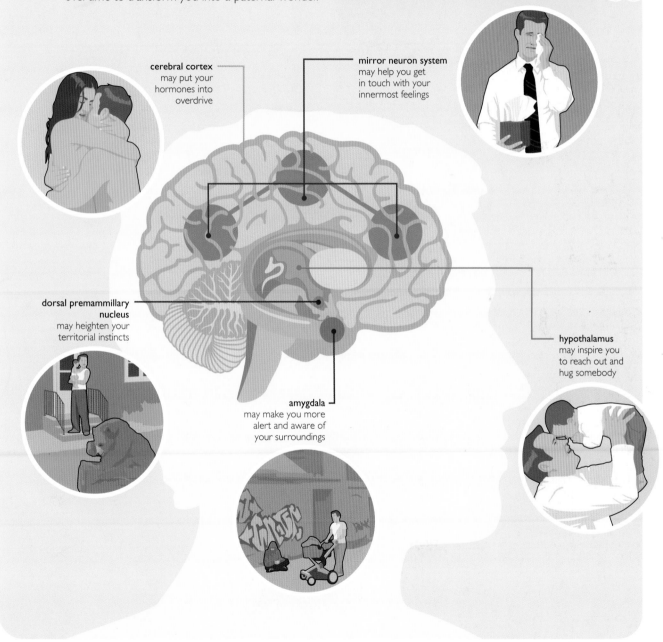

Fatherhood often increases activity in certain brain regions. Here are a few you can expect to work overtime to transform you into a paternal wonder.

cerebral cortex
may put your hormones into overdrive

mirror neuron system
may help you get in touch with your innermost feelings

dorsal premammillary nucleus
may heighten your territorial instincts

hypothalamus
may inspire you to reach out and hug somebody

amygdala
may make you more alert and aware of your surroundings

be a superdad

Do the heavy lifting.

Clean the litter box.

Help more with chores.

59 keep visits short and sweet

Monitor visitors.

Take care of emergencies.

Be supersensitive.

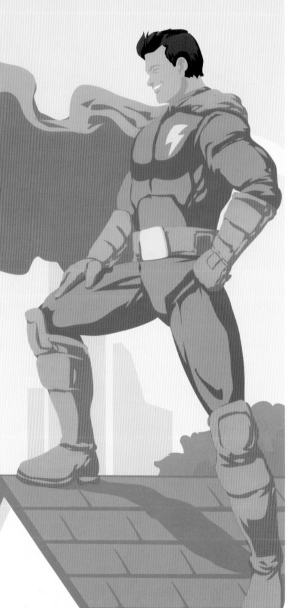

Her hair will be thicker.

Her vision may change.

Her senses will be stronger.

Her gums may be tender.

Her breasts will be amazing.

Her heartburn may increase.

She may be friskier.

Her feet may swell in size.

13 read a sonogram

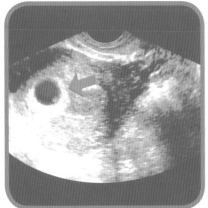
Locate the fetus.

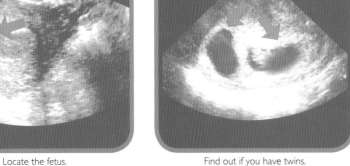
Find out if you have twins.

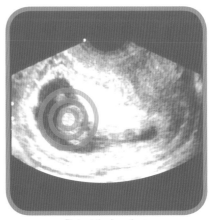
Detect the heartbeat.

14 track baby development

In nine months, your baby will grow from the size of a tiny seed to that of a football. Along the way, she'll develop vital organs and all of her extra features, like tiny toenails and tooth buds.

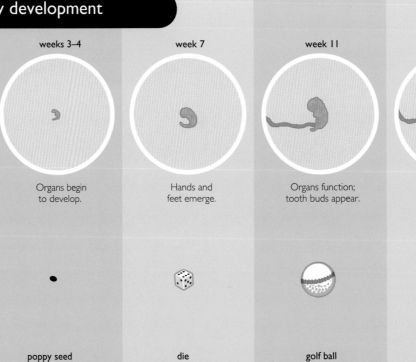

weeks 3–4	week 7	week 11	week 13
Organs begin to develop.	Hands and feet emerge.	Organs function; tooth buds appear.	Fingerprints take shape.
poppy seed 0.08 in (0.2 cm) 0.01 oz (0.3 g)	**die** 0.6 in (1.5 cm) 0.04 oz (1 g)	**golf ball** 1.6 in (4.1 cm) 0.3 oz (8.5 g)	**slider** 3 in (7.6 cm) 0.8 oz (23 g)

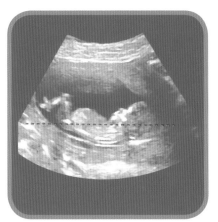

Measure to determine fetus's age.

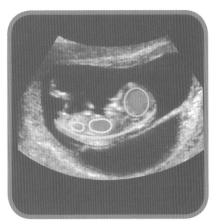

Check out organ development.

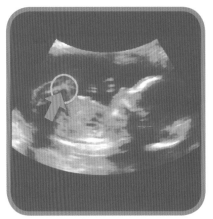

Spot gender.

week 15

Sucks thumb; taste buds form.

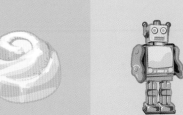

cinnamon bun
4 in (10.2 cm)
2.7 oz (76.5 g)

week 17

Has facial expressions; nails appear.

action figure
5.1 in (13 cm)
4.9 oz (139 g)

week 19

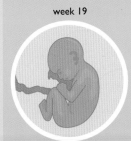

Senses develop; hair appears.

beer can
6 in (15.2 cm)
8.5 oz (241 g)

week 22

Responds to outside stimuli; eyelids form.

baseball glove
11 in (27.9 cm)
15.2 oz (431 g)

week 36

Fat layer develops; lungs ready for air.

football
18.7 in (47.5 cm)
5.8 lbs (2.6 kg)

15 make a 40-week plan

Forty weeks might sound like a long time, but the months will speed by like a teenage driver. Take care of as many details as possible now so you can focus on your new baby later.

weeks 1–4	weeks 5–8	weeks 9–12	weeks 13–16	weeks 17–20
Have sex.	Get the results.	Discuss and schedule desired prenatal tests.	Spread the news to family and friends.	Update your will or trust; buy life insurance.
Have more sex.	Determine a due date.	Share the news with your inner circle.	Admire her new curves.	Find a childbirth class.
Have even more sex.	Schedule an appointment with the doctor.	Get books on pregnancy and baby care.	Start a list of possible baby names.	Play your favorite music for baby.
Have additional sex.	Select practitioners (ob-gyn and/or midwife).	Do moderate to heavy lifting for mom.	Meet other dads-to-be.	Research big-ticket items, like a crib and stroller.

weeks 21–24	weeks 25–28	weeks 29–32	weeks 33–36	weeks 37–40
 Preregister at the hospital or birth center.	 Select a pediatrician.	 Tour the hospital or birth center.	 Prepare work colleagues for your absence.	 Learn the best route to the hospital or birth center.
 Consider a birth coach.	Decorate and organize the nursery.	 Program critical contacts into your cell phone.	 Help pack the hospital bag.	 Catch up on your sleep.
 Take an infant CPR and first-aid class.	 Read up on baby care.	 Talk about a birth plan.	 Buy and install an infant car seat.	 Get baby essentials stocked and in order.
 Make a choice about circumcision.	 Interview potential child-care providers.	Celebrate with friends and family.	Plan care for pets.	 Put on your game face.

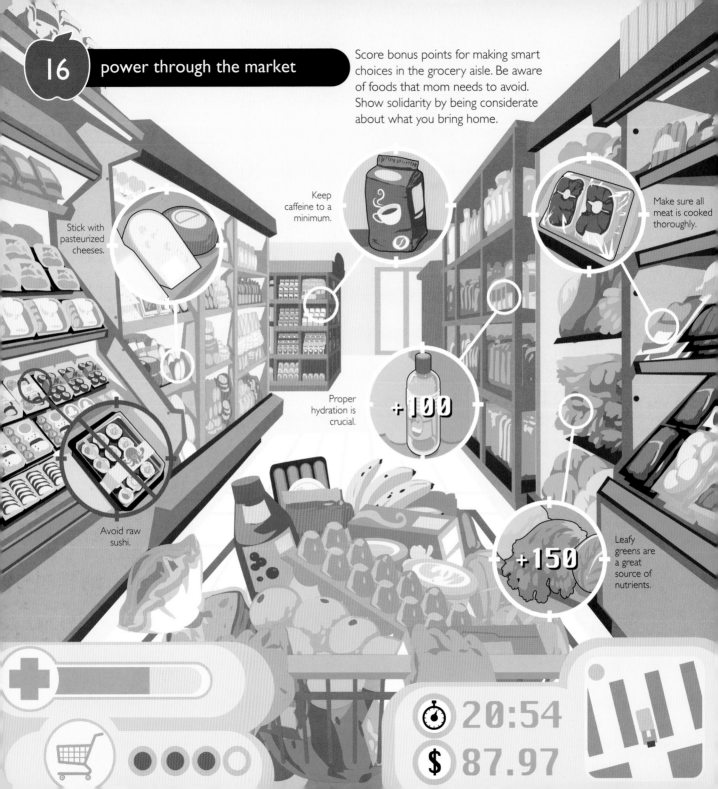

16 power through the market

Score bonus points for making smart choices in the grocery aisle. Be aware of foods that mom needs to avoid. Show solidarity by being considerate about what you bring home.

Stick with pasteurized cheeses.

Keep caffeine to a minimum.

Make sure all meat is cooked thoroughly.

Proper hydration is crucial.

+100

Avoid raw sushi.

+150

Leafy greens are a great source of nutrients.

20:54

$ 87.97

Warning: mom's cravings may be stronger than a toughman competition. Here are some healthier alternatives to common cravings, but expect that sometimes only the real thing will do.

salty snacks	herbed popcorn
ice cream	frozen yogurt
chocolate	chocolate sauce
candy	dried fruit

Champagne	sparkling cider
caffeinated soda	flavored seltzer
raw sushi	cooked or vegetable rolls
Brie	cream cheese

18 enjoy some alone time together

For the love of fallopian tubes, enjoy the limited pre-baby time you have! Make the most of it with these outings and activities.

Exercise together.

Enjoy some fine dining.

Savor your sleep.

Float your cares away.

Cheer on your team.

Bet at the track.

Win big at a carnival.

Catch a movie.

Skip scuba diving.

Avoid horseback riding.

Refuse roller coasters.

Pass on the petting zoo.

Add ice.

lemonade

lime juice

grenadine

2 Pour.

3 Shake.

4 Serve.

20 book a babymoon

Travel before 36 weeks.

Let her have the aisle seat.

Schedule daytime activities.

Enjoy time alone.

21 draw her a bath

Use warm, not hot, water.

Set the mood.

Add some bubble bath.

Scrub away any tension.

Intimacy on aisle five! Visit the local market, and you'll find a bevy of healthy foods that can fan the flames of romance.

pine nuts

carrots

chocolate-covered fruit

honey

avocados

bananas

sweet basil

pineapples

garlic

truffles

ginger

figs

almonds

Spoon.

Have her on top.

Take the pressure off.

Go manual.

Use this pre-baby time to attempt some of those things you've always wanted to do, but have been putting off. So get moving: your deadline is delivery day.

Run a marathon.

Go on a boys' retreat.

Get another degree.

Enter an eating contest.

Bet on black.

Sleep as much as possible.

Talk to a therapist.

Write your pre-baby memoir.

Record a solo album.

Try stand-up comedy.

Try out a funky hairdo.

Put a water buffalo in a trance.

Compete in a rodeo.

Create a work of art.

Learn to surf.

Train in martial arts.

Master a magic trick.

Build a ship in a bottle.

Clean the surface.

Set up your paints.

Place and trace stencil.

Paint in background; let dry.

Line up stencil.

paper towel

Dab to remove excess.

Apply paint over stencil.

Remove stencil; let dry.

Decorate with dinosaurs.

Be sweet with cupcakes.

Update with an undersea motif.

Paint on a royal crown.

Lined curtains keep room dark for napping.

Keep diaper supplies within arm's reach of the table.

A tummy strap keeps baby safe on the table.

Keep the room cool (about 68°F/ 20°C).

A fan reduces the risk of SIDS.

Set up the baby monitor 5–10 feet (1.5–3 m) from crib.

Set the garbage can within easy throwing distance.

2⅜ in (6 cm) max

Make sure the crib slats aren't too widely spaced.

Hang a mobile at least 1½ feet (0.5 m) beyond your baby's reach. Remove as soon as baby can push up on hands and knees.

The mattress should press firmly against the rails. Sheets should fit snugly. Keep blankets, toys, pillows, and crib bumpers out of the crib.

27 make wooden blocks

Mark quality pine stock.

Cut at marked increments.

Sand the entire block.

133 conquer a ninja obstacle course

Apply nontoxic paint.

28 make a mobile

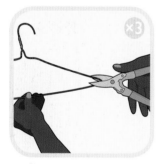

Remove the horizontal bar.

Twist up the ends.

Wrap the bar.

Arrange hangers; tape.

Color patterns and shapes.

Glue drawings to cardboard.

Attach with cables.

Hang out of reach.

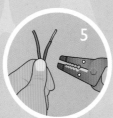

Strip the ends.

Make an underwriter's knot.

Identify the hot wire, which is smooth, and the neutral wire, which is ribbed.

Split the upper loose end of the cord.

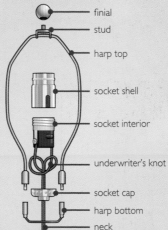

- finial
- stud
- harp top
- socket shell
- socket interior
- underwriter's knot
- socket cap
- harp bottom
- neck
- locknut
- lamp rod

Wrap the hot wire under the gold screw.

Insert the rod into the lamp base.

Wrap the neutral wire under the silver screw.

Feed the cord through the rod.

Tighten all the screws until the wires are secure.

Drill holes for the cord in the top and side of the toy. (Use a drill bit appropriate to the lamp base.)

Assemble the socket.

12 Plug in.

The key to baby-proofing is to think like a baby. Get down on the floor and crawl around for a baby's-eye view of household hazards. Repeat as your baby gets bigger and more mobile.

Place a nonslip mat in the tub.

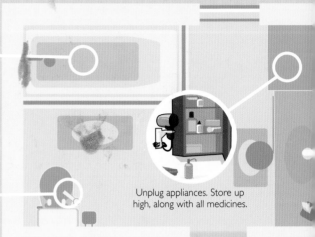

Unplug appliances. Store up high, along with all medicines.

Strap bookcases to the wall.

Install a toilet lock.

Pad sharp corners on low furniture.

Store cleaners out of reach.

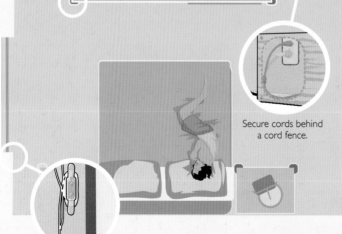

Secure cords behind a cord fence.

Set water heater to 120°F (49°C).

Tie window-blind cords out of reach.

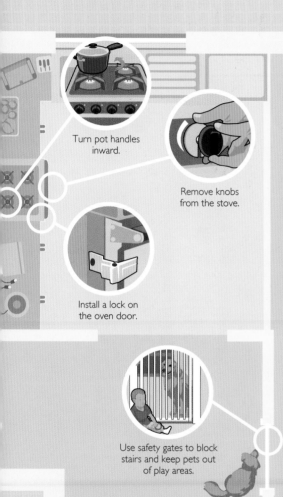

Turn pot handles
inward.

Remove knobs
from the stove.

Install a lock on
the oven door.

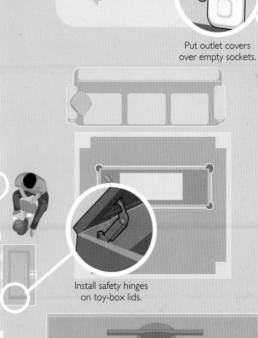

Put outlet covers
over empty sockets.

Use safety gates to block
stairs and keep pets out
of play areas.

Install safety hinges
on toy-box lids.

If an item fits
through a toilet
paper tube, keep
it out of reach! If
it's smaller than
1¾ inches (4.5 cm)
in diameter, it's a
choking hazard.

Secure breakables
on high shelves.

Say it on a stein.

Send a signal into the sky.

Wear it with pride.

Brand a steak.

Shout it from the roof.

Try viral marketing.

Carve it in the crops.

Get a tattoo.

Start a college fund.

With the pregnancy moving by swiftly and free time at a premium, make it your mission to keep friends and family informed. A blog is a great way to update the masses.

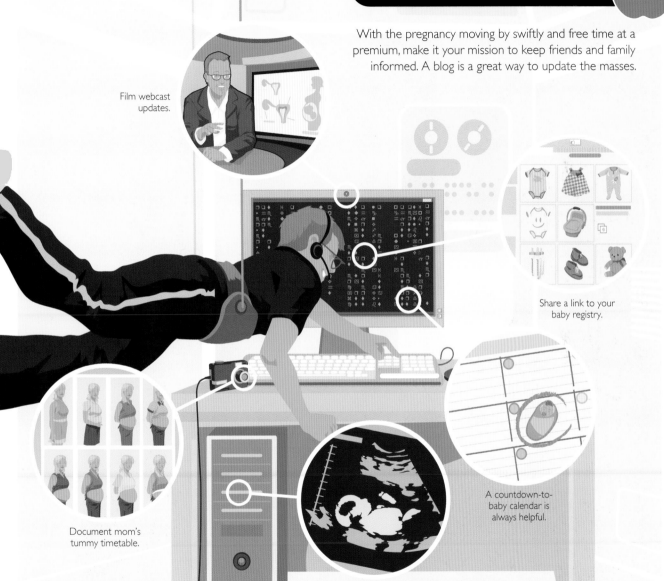

Film webcast updates.

Share a link to your baby registry.

A countdown-to-baby calendar is always helpful.

Document mom's tummy timetable.

Show off the latest sonogram.

0 to 12 months   12 to 24 months   sleep safe travel friendly

includes stroller and car seat

canopy provides sun protection

ample room for storing items

travel system

light and compact

limited storage space

easy to maneuver in tight spaces

umbrella stroller

promotes bonding

baby's head and face should be visible at all times

easy to use

baby sling

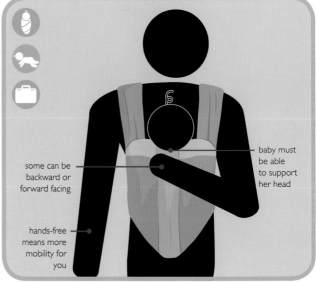

some can be backward or forward facing

hands-free means more mobility for you

baby must be able to support her head

baby carrier

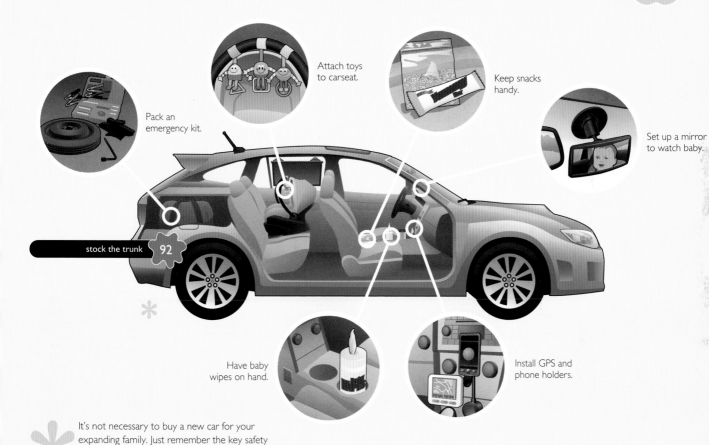

Pack an emergency kit.

Attach toys to carseat.

Keep snacks handy.

Set up a mirror to watch baby.

stock the trunk **92**

Have baby wipes on hand.

Install GPS and phone holders.

It's not necessary to buy a new car for your expanding family. Just remember the key safety features and look into easy ways to trick out your car to make it the ultimate baby-mobile.

minivan

✔ Room for growing families.
✔ Sliding doors for easy access.
✔ Must leave cool status behind.

sport utility vehicle

✔ Solid crash protection.
✔ Participation in sports not necessary.
✔ Check models for fuel economy.

sedan

✔ Gets good gas mileage.
✔ Easy to park.
✔ Less storage for baby gear.

35 name your baby

Look to the family tree.

Consider the meaning.

Ponder your heritage.

Explore history.

No matter where you find a name, be sure to test it out before you seal the deal. How well does it fit with baby's last name? Does it have a good rhythm when you say it out loud?

36 find a pediatrician

Ask friends and family.

Narrow down your choices.

Check your insurance.

Identify affiliated hospitals.

Find inspiration in nature.

Think globally.

Point to pop culture.

Go for the unique.

Keep away from car names.

Avoid alcoholic inspiration.

No pet namesakes.

Ax out exes.

Look into office hours.

Inspect the waiting room.

Check after-hours policies.

Meet with the doctor.

make your baby stand out

Let's face facts, no one wants to be seen with a boring baby. These items can jazz up any ensemble and make your baby the life of the party.

team jersey

sweet shades

rocking one piece

big-boy cargos

132 hang out with baby

frilly tutu

supercool kicks

mohawk madness

mitten mania

38

create a custom iron-on

 + + +

Choose an image.

Use iron-on paper to print.

Iron on the iron-on.

Show off your creation.

Studies show that babies recognize voices and music that they heard before they were born. When choosing music, consider classical and save the Swedish death metal for the tween years. Touch can be a great way to bond too. Gentle taps and massages will draw the whole family together.

Give mom and baby a light massage.

Listening to your baby's heartbeat can make you feel instantly connected.

Share your favorite tunes with baby.

Read out loud. Babies show a preference for voices they hear in utero.

Invite loved ones to talk to baby. Their familiar voices will be soothing later.

When mom feels baby being active, tap a rhythm and wait for a response.

40 spot the approach of labor

She's nesting.

Her back may ache.

Her water breaks.

Contractions are regular.

41 dress for the hospital

At the hospital, you will fulfill the role of press secretary, family liaison, and errand runner. You'll also have a lot of downtime with mom and baby. These two looks will work for any situation.

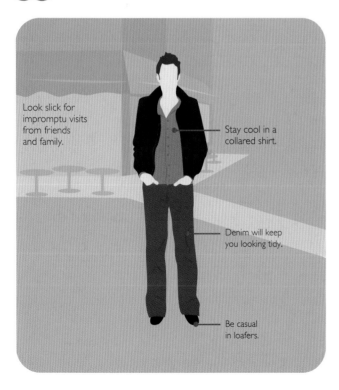

Look slick for impromptu visits from friends and family.

Stay cool in a collared shirt.

Denim will keep you looking tidy.

Be casual in loafers.

Be comfortable while helping mom and hanging out in the hospital.

Break out an old t-shirt.

Stroll the halls in shorts.

Slip on flip-flops.

When you head to the hospital, you'll both want some comforts from home. Pack a small, easy-to-carry bag for the mom-to-be, and a separate bag for larger items (and for all of your manly needs).

outfit for baby

exercise ball

contact list

map of hospital area

cell phone and charger

cash and coins for vending machines

massage oil and tennis ball

MP3 player and dock

diaper bag

grooming items

shampoo and deodorant

toothpaste and toothbrushes

watch

snacks

car seat

deck of cards

camera and batteries

laptop

dad-to-be

shampoo and deodorant

hard candy

reading material

sanitary pads

eyewear and supplies

lip balm

soap and hand lotion

hair-care items

nursing bra

labor clothes

robe and slippers

medical documents

extra underwear

clothes to wear home

slip-on shoes

mom-to-be

Your challenge: master the best route to the hospital. Don't leave important details to chance. Doing your recon and area surveillance in advance will save you a lot of time and stress.

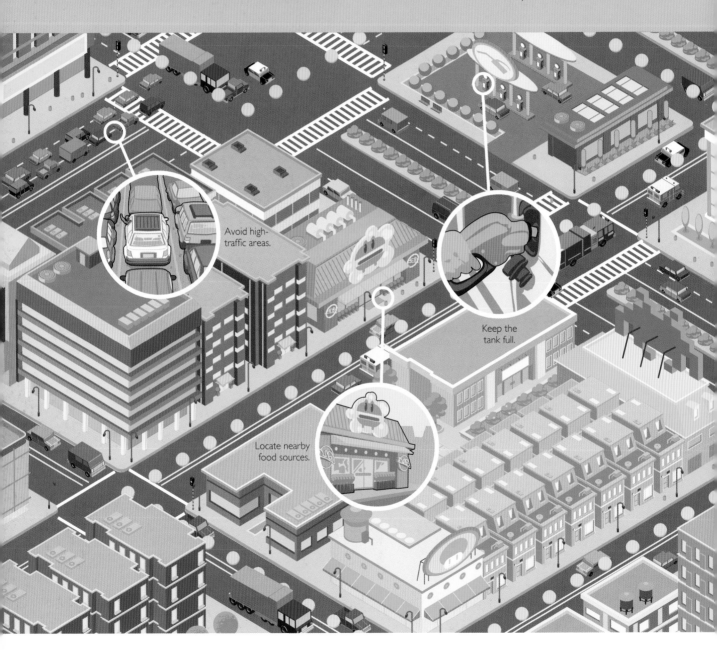

Avoid high-traffic areas.

Keep the tank full.

Locate nearby food sources.

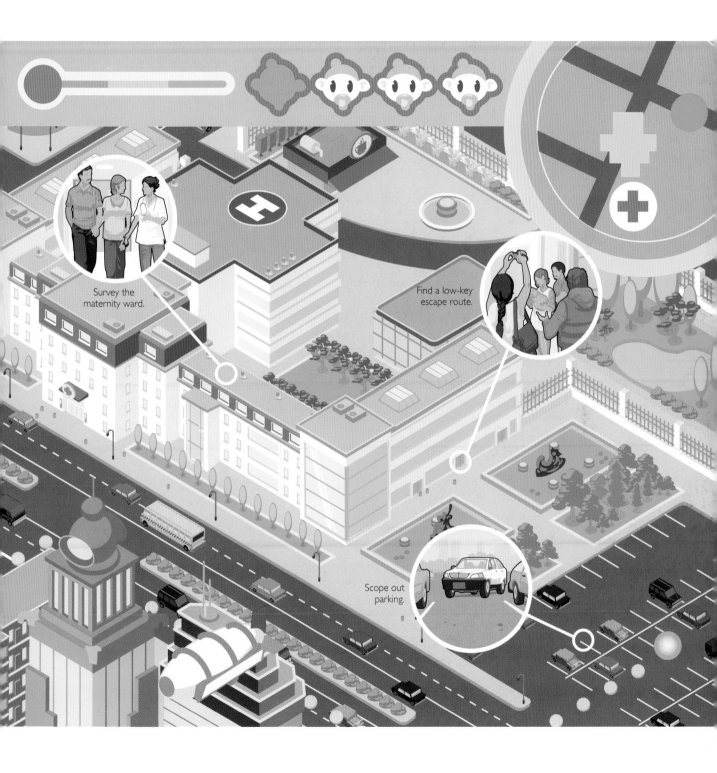

Survey the
maternity ward.

Find a low-key
escape route.

Scope out
parking.

Imagine being hired as a pilot with no training. "Here's the cockpit. Good luck getting us to Houston." That's what it's like coming home with a newborn. The challenges come fast and furious, and just as one is resolved, another pops up. Here's a typical scenario: baby spits up on himself. *Whoa! Why did that happen?* Before putting him in a clean outfit, you change his diaper. *Wait a second…is poo supposed to be that color?* As you attempt to get flailing arms through pajama sleeves, baby is complaining loudly, and dressing him is making him even crankier. *Am I doing this wrong?* Situations like this can lead to Ming vase syndrome, when dad is afraid to handle baby for fear of breaking him. Luckily knowledge is the cure, and the first dose is on the next page.

deal

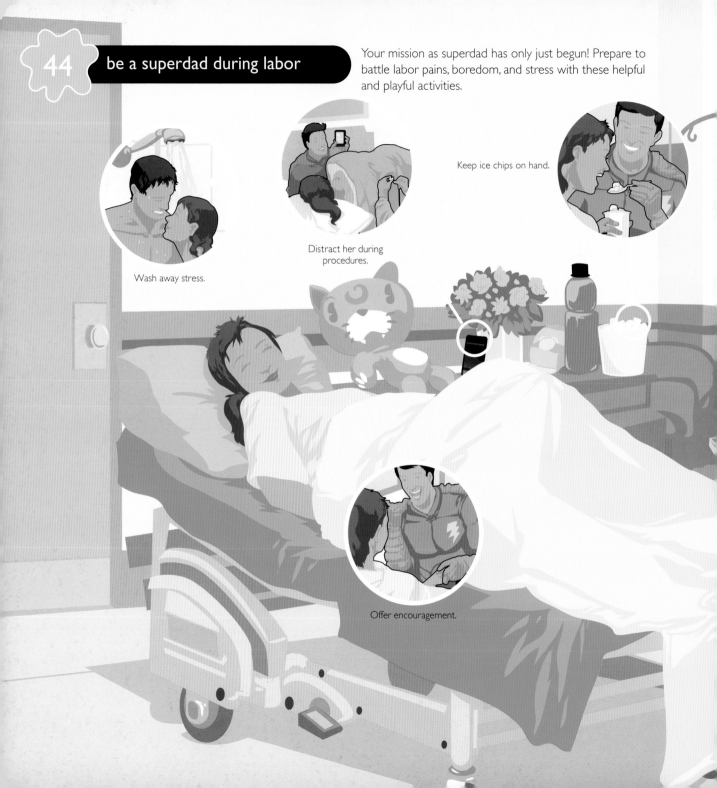

be a superdad during labor

Your mission as superdad has only just begun! Prepare to battle labor pains, boredom, and stress with these helpful and playful activities.

Keep ice chips on hand.

Distract her during procedures.

Wash away stress.

Offer encouragement.

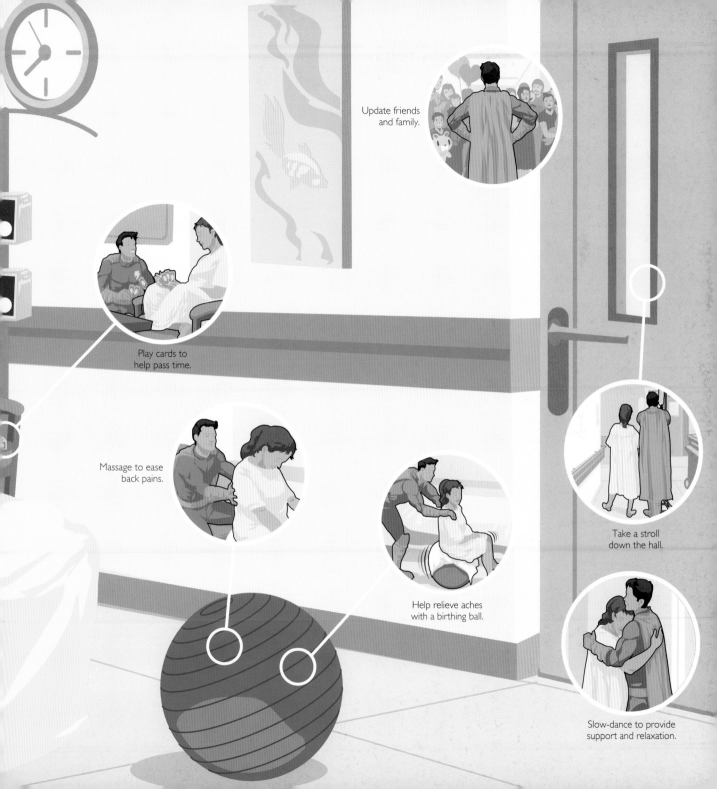

Update friends and family.

Play cards to help pass time.

Massage to ease back pains.

Help relieve aches with a birthing ball.

Take a stroll down the hall.

Slow-dance to provide support and relaxation.

contractions		dilation	tips

early

15–20 minutes apart	Last 30–45 seconds	Dilation begins	Alert the doctor. Practice breathing exercises. Encourage mom to walk.
5 minutes apart	Last 30–45 seconds	4 cm	Call close family and friends. Go to the hospital. Don't panic.

active

3 minutes apart	Last 60 seconds	4–8 cm	Suggest pain-management options. Early in this phase, don't be surprised if the hospital sends her home.

transition

2–3 minutes apart	Last 60–90 seconds	10 cm	Be extra sympathetic—her pain level is at its highest now. Get ready to meet baby.

An epidural might be given to ease discomfort.

Support during pushing with breathing exercises.

Prepare for arrival.

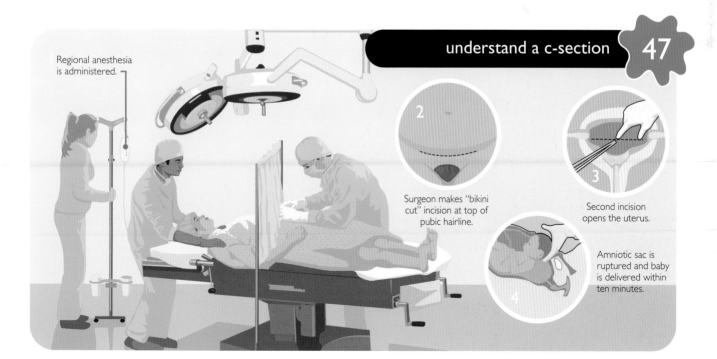

Regional anesthesia is administered.

Surgeon makes "bikini cut" incision at top of pubic hairline.

Second incision opens the uterus.

Amniotic sac is ruptured and baby is delivered within ten minutes.

Locate the next major stop.

Use gravity to help.

Gently catch baby.

Wipe baby's face.

Tie off the umbilical cord.

Hold close and keep warm.

Breast-feed if possible.

Exit to street level.

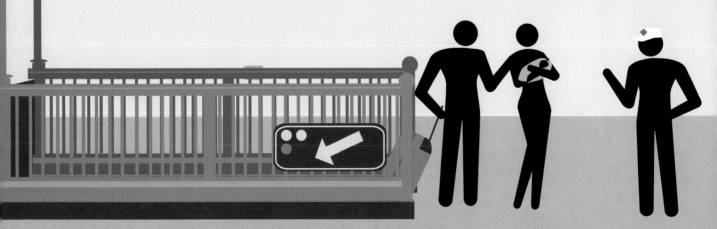

engage in an elevator delivery 49

Use soothing music to relax mom.

Hit the "alarm" button.

make a musical entrance 50

Make sure to buy baby a concert t-shirt.

Pass her to the medic station.

go for a game-show birth 51

Start college fund immediately!

Name baby after the host.

deliver during the apocalypse 52

Avoid a zombie midwife.

Don't worry about any mess.

Don't be alarmed if your newborn arrives with some unexpected fuzz, bumps, or marks.

lanugo
Downy back, limb, and shoulder fuzz will disappear in a few days.

mongolian spots
These bruise-like blotches are harmless melanin spots.

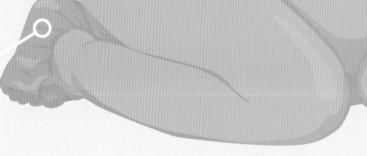

discoloration
Blue hands and feet should turn rosy as baby's circulation strengthens, but check in with your doctor if this persists.

swelling
Swollen breasts and genitals are the result of mom's hormones.

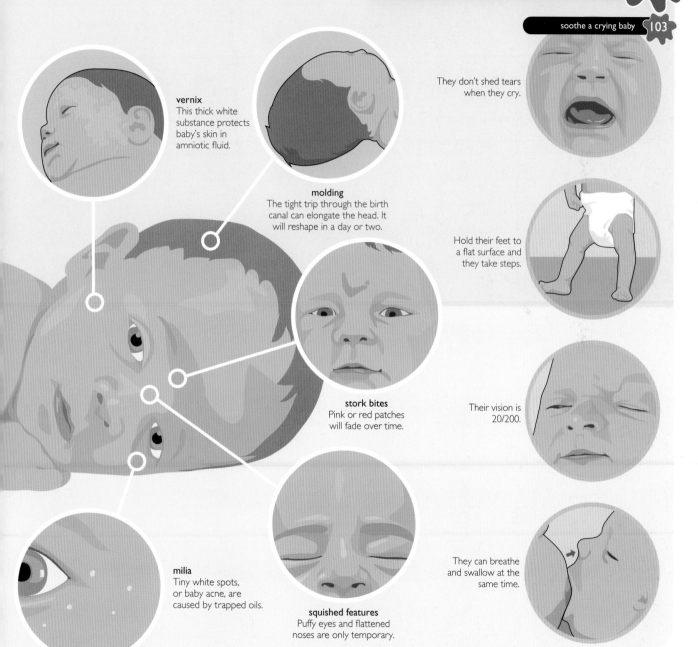

vernix
This thick white substance protects baby's skin in amniotic fluid.

molding
The tight trip through the birth canal can elongate the head. It will reshape in a day or two.

They don't shed tears when they cry.

Hold their feet to a flat surface and they take steps.

stork bites
Pink or red patches will fade over time.

Their vision is 20/200.

milia
Tiny white spots, or baby acne, are caused by trapped oils.

squished features
Puffy eyes and flattened noses are only temporary.

They can breathe and swallow at the same time.

55 announce the news by air

Welcome to the world, Baby Ann

56 make a halftime proclamation

IT'S A GIRL!

57 toast to your new baby

58 inform the neighborhood

IT'S A BOY!

Ask visitors to wash up.

Place baby in waiting arms.

Lay baby in little laps.

Invite children to touch toes.

Expose pet to other babies.

Offer baby's clothes for a sniff.

Greet pet; bring in baby.

Hold baby; reassure pet.

Cradle hold makes rocking baby easy.

Football hold keeps an arm free.

120 tackle tummy time

Belly hold counts as tummy time.

Shoulder hold is good for walking.

62 swaddle a baby

Swaddling, also known as the "baby burrito," can pacify your little one in the first couple months by reminding her of the snug, warm environment of the womb.

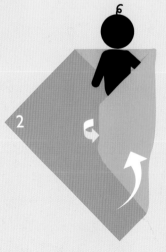

Beware the boombox hold.

Don't dare do the dangle.

Keep away from the tuck.

Avoid the bag carry.

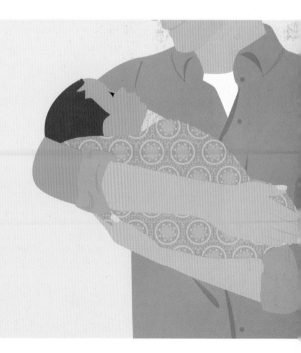

Babies have personalities and mood swings just like adults. Start with one and collect them all!

"Nervous" Pervis Wilhelm

"Fussy" Russ Perez

Jill "the Chill" Bullock

CAREER HIGHLIGHTS

Strangers scare him.

Gets you out of family gatherings.

Cries when the doorbell rings.

Insider tip: he'll be less fussy hanging out in smaller groups of people.

CAREER HIGHLIGHTS

Wriggles off grandma's lap.

Is known to throw empty sippy cups.

Is very clear about what he wants.

Insider tip: don't let him get bored. Keep him moving and narrate what's going on.

CAREER HIGHLIGHTS

Socializes easily at the neighborhood picnic.

Can fall asleep near a construction zone.

Will eat anything and everything.

Insider tip: keep her engaged but don't overwhelm her with physical activity.

Babies can't speak, so they use sounds and body language to communicate. Look for these telltale baby cues.

I'm overstimulated.

gaze aversion

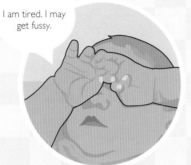

I am tired. I may get fussy.

rubbing eyes

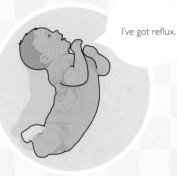

I've got reflux.

arching back

I'm scared. Swaddle me.

startle reflex

Let's have a chat.

cooing

I may be pooping.

concentrating face

I'm uncomfortable.

pain cry

Feed me now!

hunger cry

Sometimes the sounds are as important as the body language. The pain cry is long and loud, with a sustained pitch. The hunger cry is short and low-pitched.

65 — hang with a hipster dad

Spends excessively on baby gear.

Dresses baby cooler than most adults.

Turns punk songs into lullabies.

66 — spot a nervous dad

Constantly asks for child-care advice.

Overstocks diaper bag.

Lingers at day-care drop-off.

67 — chill with an eco dad

Smells strongly of patchouli.

Outfits nursery with all-natural products.

Makes his own organic baby food.

68 — play with a big-kid dad

Does great voices at storytime.

May crowd the sandbox.

Can be prone to playground injuries.

Surprise her with treats.

Bring her flowers.

Help with chores.

Serenade her.

give mom a break 70

 +

Plan an afternoon for moms.

Organize with other dads.

Give them the day off.

enjoy a daddy playdate 125

Chill with the gang.

use a phone to be a better dad

Keep track of appointments.

Check your grocery list.

Send messages to baby while away.

Soothe baby with the music player.

Use the GPS function to stay on track.

Show off your pictures everywhere.

rig a phone as a baby monitor

Call your phone.

Place by baby.

Plug in earpiece and turn up.

Stay tuned in.

use your phone to escape

Record household drama.

Set a discreet phone alarm.

Stand next to the host.

Answer the alarm.

Check your voice mail.

Agree to leave.

Apologize and exit.

Reuse as needed.

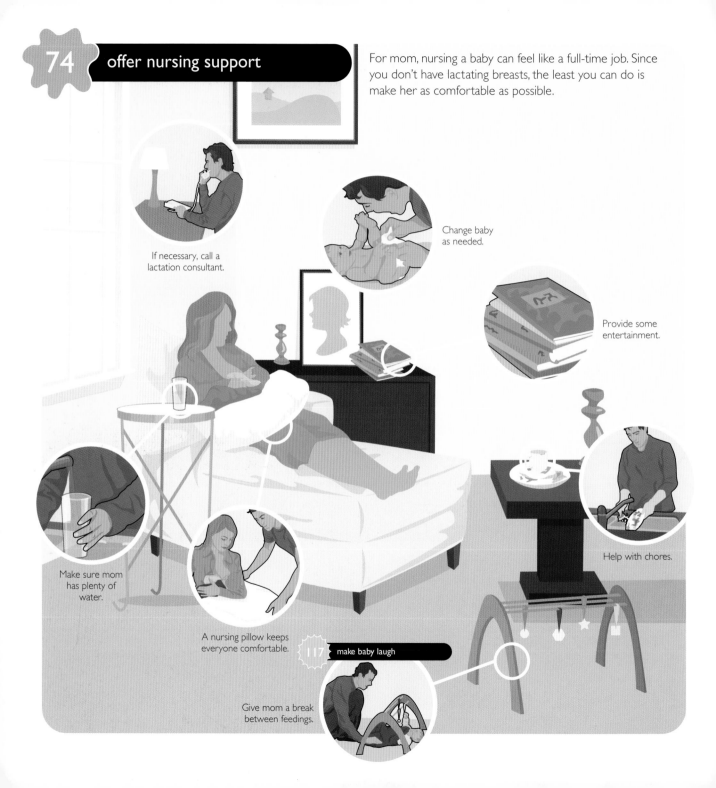

For mom, nursing a baby can feel like a full-time job. Since you don't have lactating breasts, the least you can do is make her as comfortable as possible.

If necessary, call a lactation consultant.

Change baby as needed.

Provide some entertainment.

Make sure mom has plenty of water.

Help with chores.

A nursing pillow keeps everyone comfortable.

117 ▸ make baby laugh

Give mom a break between feedings.

Keep baby's head up.

Burp baby frequently.

Keep baby upright.

Watch baby's cues.

No matter how careful you are, spit-ups will happen. Keep a burp cloth handy and don't freak out. Most babies grow out of it in the first six months.

Place a burp cloth.

Position baby.

Rub or pat baby's back . . .

. . . until burp is achieved!

Don't worry if your baby doesn't burp every time. If she hasn't burped after four minutes, she may not need to, so feel free to stop.

77 mix formula the right way

Use purified water.

Stir, don't shake.

Prepare single servings only.

Feed baby.

When it's stored properly, frozen breast milk will last for three to six months. Thawed milk must be used within 24 hours. Fresh breast milk will keep in the refrigerator for five days.

78 store and thaw breast milk

Double-bag breast milk.

Freeze.

Thaw in warm water.

Stir milk to distribute heat.

Sterilize before initial use.

Check the flow rate.

Be sure milk is warm, not hot.

Hold the bottle, don't prop.

Angle to avoid air bubbles.

Burp during and after meal.

Alternate sides.

Wash in dishwasher or sink.

Replace nipple when worn.

1 Lay baby on a flat surface. Strap him in if possible.

2 Keep him covered to avoid being sprayed.

3 Wipe down, collecting mess.

4 Set diaper aside.

5 Keep feet and bottom elevated.

6 Wipe from front to back; don't forget skin folds.

7 Tuck used wipes in messy diaper.

8 Place fresh diaper under baby; apply cream as needed.

9 Secure diaper; fit should be snug, not tight.

10 Seal the mess for disposal.

Is that color normal? Don't freak out! Baby's poo will come in a variety of colors that differ from our own and change over time.

dark green
the color of meconium,
baby's first poo

mustard yellow
the typical color for
breast-fed babies

yellow with hints of green
the typical color for
formula-fed babies

red
could be harmless blood
remnants or a serious matter;
check with your pediatrician

white
a rarity but may be the sign
of a liver problem;
check with your pediatrician

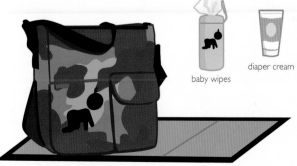

baby wipes

diaper cream

spare clothes
and blankets

toy

pacifier

bottles

diaper bag and changing mat

two diapers for each
hour, plus extras

plastic bags

book

snacks for
older babies

Disinfect any soiled surfaces.

Change her diaper while she's standing up.

Keep a bucket of soapy water nearby.

Blowouts? Try a larger diaper or switch brands.

Improvise a changing station.

Contain a mess by using your coat to swaddle.

Put a larger diaper over a smaller one.

Use tape to keep baby's diaper closed.

Sweet foods can lead to digestive problems.

Buff your car with too-small diapers.

Baby sunblock is great for sensitive skin.

Reuse diaper bag as a laptop bag.

Baby wipes are handy for wiping down the dashboard.

Baby-food jars are great for storing small items.

Baby oil can help unstick a zipper.

A superdad is always resourceful. When supplies are low, he knows where to find amazing substitutes among common baby items.

Cure hangovers with electrolyte replacements.

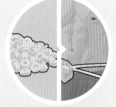

Baby snacks are tasty, low-calorie, low-fat food.

85 sponge-bathe a newborn

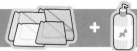

Wipe face from nose out.

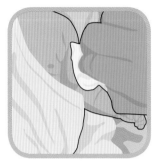

Clean all skin folds.

Get between toes.

Shampoo with damp cloth.

86 bathe a baby

Prepare tub; gather supplies.

Support head and back.

Wash face first.

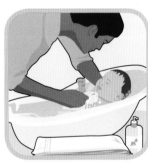

Wash body top to bottom.

Add water to prevent chills.

Lean her over to wash back.

Wash her hair last.

Dry and dress.

clip nails safely 87

Wait for a calm moment.

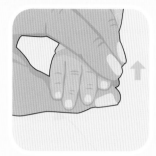

Press pad away from nail.

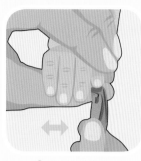

Cut a curved shape.

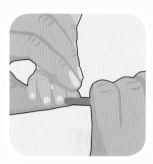

File any ragged edges.

prevent diaper rash 88

 To clean, use unscented wipes or plain water. See your doctor for severe rashes.

Change diaper frequently.

Clean well and pat dry.

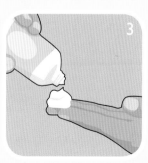

Use cream often.

Air out any flare-ups.

When it comes to clothes, keeping him safe and comfortable is always the hottest trend. So style that child the right way.

Read tags for size.

Pull hands through sleeves.

Avoid drawstrings.

Skip studded or bejeweled items.

Check elastic for fit.

Put finger under zipper.

Dress baby in layers.

Footie pajamas simplify life.

baking soda

meat tenderizer

lemon juice

white vinegar

nail polish remover

rubbing alcohol

sunshine

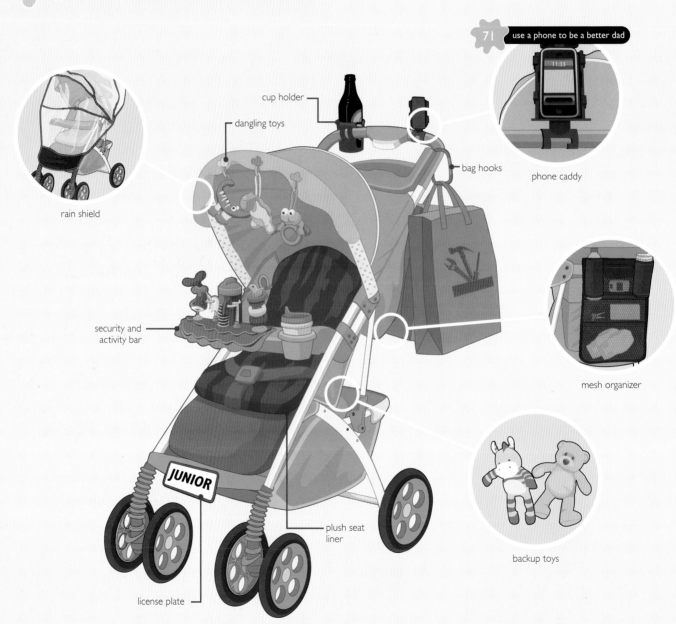

71 use a phone to be a better dad

cup holder

dangling toys

bag hooks

phone caddy

rain shield

security and
activity bar

mesh organizer

plush seat
liner

JUNIOR

license plate

backup toys

umbrella

diaper cream

sunblock

wet wipes

diapers

market bags

extra clothes

trash bags

outdoor toys

baby wipes

indoor toys

blankets

bottled water

first-aid kit

Use an approved car seat.

Check stroller at the gate.

Pack extra supplies.

Feed at takeoff.

Change in the bathroom.

Distract with new toys.

Take a walk if she's upset.

Feed during descent.

94 distract baby at the store

Stimulate her senses by letting her smell and touch safe items.

1

Name the items you are buying. Talk about what you are doing.

Let baby drop unbreakables into the basket.

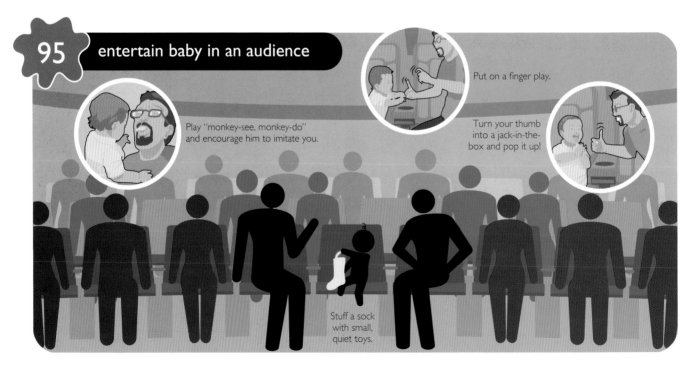

95 entertain baby in an audience

Put on a finger play.

Play "monkey-see, monkey-do" and encourage him to imitate you.

Turn your thumb into a jack-in-the-box and pop it up!

Stuff a sock with small, quiet toys.

Play a naming game. Ask him to point to parts of his face or body.

Hold him close and hum a tune.

Entertain baby with a clapping game.

Hide a small toy in your pocket or sleeve and play hide-and-seek.

Bring a toy phone so he can catch up on important calls.

Unplug the keyboard and let him push buttons.

Hand over your keys.

Help him crinkle waste paper and put it into the recycling bin.

Flip the couch cushions.

Vacuum a quick path.

Air out the house.

Stuff the laundry room.

Hide dirty dishes.

Wipe down the sink.

Stash items in the shower.

Use baby as distraction.

99 make a baby mop

Cut up your mop.

Use nontoxic glue.

Press mop pieces down.

Let baby go!

Takeout and delivery can be unhealthy for your body and your wallet. A rotisserie chicken is a great start for a simple, healthy meal you can make in minutes.

rotisserie chicken

bbq sauce

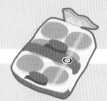

burger buns

bbq chicken sandwich

croutons

caesar salad mix

chicken caesar salad

tortillas

cheese

salsa

chicken quesadillas

snack on a pita pizza 141

english muffins

tomato sauce

cheese

english muffin pizzas

cranberry sauce

stuffing

classic dinner

101   dine out with baby

Choose family-friendly spots.

Avoid peak mealtimes.

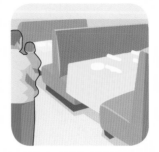

Request a booth, if possible.

Buckle up for safety.

102   deal with a fussy eater

Throw down a drop cloth.

Strap baby in his seat.

Cover up clothes.

Use two spoons.

Make a safe zone.

Bring baby's food and drink.

Pack quiet distractions.

Keep a favorite toy on hand.

Offer a sippy cup.

Serve small bites.

Let him be picky.

No luck? Try again later.

103 soothe a crying baby

See if she needs a change.

Make sure clothes are loose.

Change location; go outside.

Sway to music.

Run vacuum (or dryer).

61 hold a baby

Try a new hold.

Hold her close; hum a tune.

Try some mirror magic.

104 troubleshoot an infant's sleep

Create some white noise.

Prewarm baby's bed.

Swaddle in familiar scents.

Keep him upright.

Start at the same time.

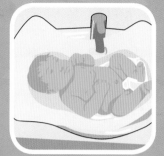

Soothe with a warm bath.

Fill baby's belly.

Change wet or dirty diapers.

Darken the room.

Sing a lullaby.

Lay on back; pat gently.

Use your ritual anywhere.

 You may get a little tired of doing the same thing, but a consistent bedtime ritual signals to your baby that it's time for sleep and can help him settle down for the night. Once you've established your own pattern, try to stick with it.

We know, we know: you're as tired as, well, a new parent. Baby's erratic sleep patterns have your normal snoozing schedule turned upside down, and taking the day off is not an option. Luckily there are tricks that can make it easier.

Pull over if you can't stay awake.

Don't get too comfy.

Listen to loud music.

Chew gum.

Painted eyelids won't fool anyone.

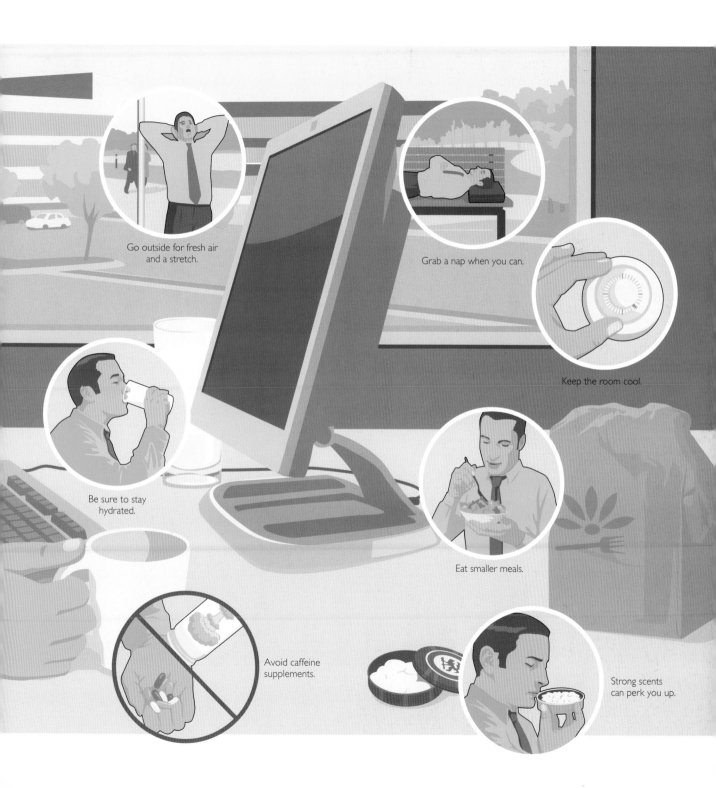

Go outside for fresh air and a stretch.

Grab a nap when you can.

Keep the room cool.

Be sure to stay hydrated.

Eat smaller meals.

Avoid caffeine supplements.

Strong scents can perk you up.

The world is your personal trainer! From parks to playgrounds, the opportunities for exercise and activity are everywhere. Plus, fresh air will do both you and baby good.

chin-ups
No bar handy? Use sturdy tree branches to tone your arms.

angled push-ups
Find a well-anchored object that's about waist height.

triceps dips
Raise and lower yourself from a fixed, raised object.

squats
Hold this position against a tree.

hamstring stretches
Kick your leg up to stretch before and after exercising.

side planks
You can strike this ab-strengthening pose on any level surface.

bicycle
Find an elevated surface for ab-toning "bicycle" moves.

love the stroller lunge 108

practice peekaboo crunches 109

build your biceps with baby 110

twist with your toddler 111

+ +

Chocolate, oysters, infants: which one of these is not an aphrodisiac? Post-baby romance can be a difficult path to navigate, but doing so is good for everyone. Sex relieves stress and boosts immunity. But be patient: mom needs time to adjust and feel sexy again.

Think sparklers, not fireworks.

Be understanding.

Take a cold shower.

Keep your brain occupied.

Shower her with compliments.

Stay sexy.

Wait four to six weeks.

Make the most of nap time.

Use a personal lubricant.

Birth control is a must.

Breasts may be off limits.

Laugh off any awkwardness.

Playtime can happen just about anywhere: the grocery store, the airport, or the front yard. And it can happen fast: *a laundry basket becomes a rocket in 1.3 seconds!* Another great thing about playtime: it's really very simple. You don't need toys that teach six languages or fire flash-card rockets. Things like balls, boxes, bubbles, or just your smile do the trick just fine. And did we mention the amazing benefits? Did you know that play can promote motor skills, improve concentration and memory, and nurture social development and imagination? There are some real perks for dad too. This is the only time that a grown man can act like a horse, a ninja, and a pirate all in the same day. Everyone wins!

play

| | 0–3 months | 3+ months | 6+ months | 9+ months |

rippling ribbons
boosts visual tracking and eye-hand coordination

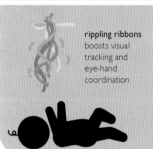

airplane ride
eases colic; develops neck and shoulder strength

hammock time
promotes balance; builds back and neck strength

noisemakers
fosters sound location; teaches cause and effect

rolling a ball
develops balance and coordination

nature walk
provides sensory experiences

knocking blocks
refines motor skills; promotes shape recognition

pillow obstacle course
nurtures body awareness; strengthens eye-foot coordination

Lend a hand.

Put temptation out of reach.

Place toys at 10:00 and 2:00.

Make a tunnel.

12+ months	18+ months	24+ months	30+ months

bubble chase
boosts eye-hand coordination; gives tactile stimulation

sand play
advances fine motor skills; provides tactile stimulation

kid-directed puppet show
nurtures imagination; aids language development and social skills

magnifying glass
teaches cause and effect; enriches visual experience

mimic game
encourages social bonding; builds body awareness

sealed plastic jar rattles
promotes creative movement; cultivates rhythm

bathtime pouring
teaches problem-solving; enhances fine motor skills

playing dress-up
encourages creativity; develops social skills

encourage walking **116**

Give her something to push.

Support her torso; cheer!

Take off her shoes.

Shine light for her to chase.

Make faces and silly sounds.

Drop soft toys by baby.

Taste and tickle baby's toes.

Blow raspberries.

Hide most of your body.

Search for musical toys.

Guess which cup.

Put a lid on a container.

Hide toy behind your back.

Cover toy with a towel.

Play with a mirror.

Peekaboo!

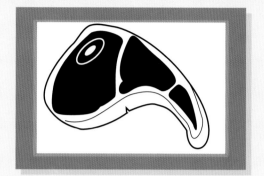

Babies find high-contrast images like these visually stimulating.
Hang simple black-and-white pictures where baby can get a
look. Provide baby with brightly colored toys too.

Slowly wave bright toys.

stencil with style 25

Hang high-contrast art.

Wear stripes!

Slowly pull a toy past baby.

Prop baby up for a better view.

Position something for her to look at.

Get belly to belly.

Give her a leg up.

Lie down for some face time.

Drape baby over your arm.

Tummy time builds neck and torso strength. Your baby may find tummy time more enjoyable if she can look around, so try propping her up. If she's still cranky, try again later.

shape up with a sit-up 121

1 Lay baby on your legs, holding his hands.

2 Let him pull up (with your help) to build core muscles.

practice the rollover 122

1 Place baby on a blanket or towel.

2 Lift the edge under his shoulder slowly.

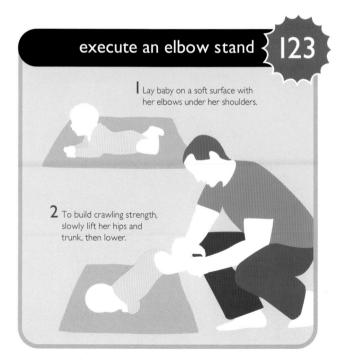

execute an elbow stand 123

1 Lay baby on a soft surface with her elbows under her shoulders.

2 To build crawling strength, slowly lift her hips and trunk, then lower.

work out the wheelbarrow 124

1 Wait until baby can lift her head and prop herself up on her arms.

2 Support her trunk and legs; hold for a slow count of three.

When baby can hold his head upright, he can swing.

A rolled-up blanket or jacket behind baby adds support.

148 } grow and learn with bubbles

Play bubble chase with beginning walkers.

Help baby climb stairs to build coordination.

Fill and spill buckets or bury toys in the sand for baby to find.

Guide baby down the slide.

Bring extra toys to ease sharing issues.

To avoid injury, don't slide together.

Always slide down feet first.

Make sure the slide isn't too hot.

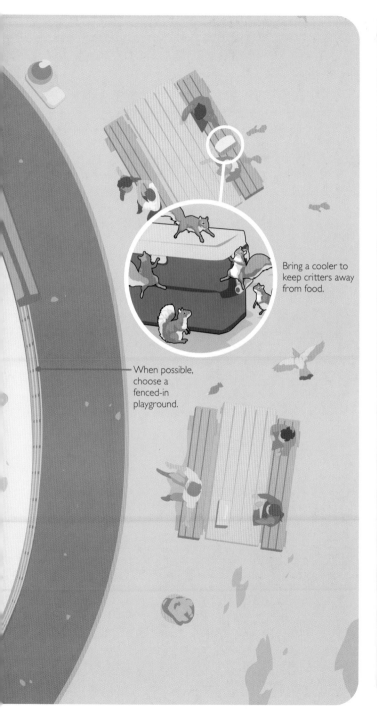

Bring a cooler to keep critters away from food.

When possible, choose a fenced-in playground.

Wear a hat to ease sun glare.

Stock a bag with snacks, toys, and sunblock.

Cargo shorts add instant storage.

Sneakers will help you keep up with baby.

127 **build language skills**

Repeat consonant sounds.

Make eye contact; mimic.

Narrate your actions.

Use gestures.

Name the things you see.

Count.

Ask questions.

Play phone; repeat words.

128 **teach baby sign language**

Bunch fingers, tap mouth.

Tip a pretend cup to mouth.

Bunch fingers; tap hands.

Tap head with open hand.

Sit facing your baby.

Hold under his arms.

Ask if the flight crew is ready.

Three, two, one . . .

Count down for takeoff.

Roll back to lift off.

Keep eye contact.

Bring him in for a landing.

Repeat.

Hold baby securely.

Lift her up.

Gently swing to the right.

Gently swing to the left.

Everyday household items make fantastic toys.
With some imagination, your little monster
can have a smashing good time.

Stomp paper bag buildings.

Cause a container crash.

Do a rolling derby.

Have a sock hop.

Knock down a block tower.

Take a laundry basket cruise.

Play the pots and pans.

150 build boxcars and more

Build a box fort.

Take in a game.

Enjoy the great outdoors.

Rock out at a concert.

Stroll down the midway.

Join a parade.

Bring her to a convention.

Play at the science museum.

Meet animals at the zoo.

conquer a ninja obstacle course

Start with a bow.

Weave with stealth.

Kick away obstacles.

Sneak into the fortress.

observe movement milestones

As civilization progressed through the ages, so will your baby's mobility increase…but luckily a lot faster. This is a general guide to some movement milestones; keep in mind that your baby will learn to walk and crawl at her own pace.

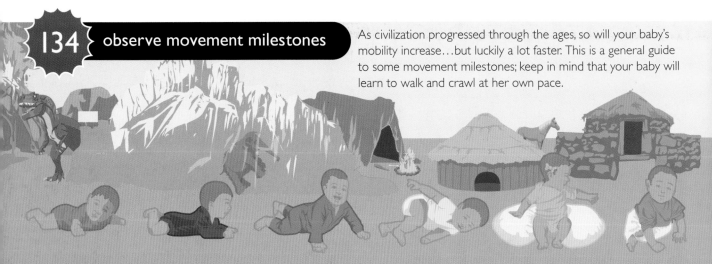

month 1
holds her head up
from flat surface

months 2–3
leans on her forearms
to lift head

month 3
pushes her head
and chest up

months 3–4
rolls from her tummy
to her back

months 4–5
sits supported

months 5–6
sits on her own

Climb the impossible peak.

Topple the tower of toys.

Karate-chop cookie.

Collect your reward.

months 6–11
moves forward by scooting, creeping, or crawling

months 7–10
pulls up; walks holding on to furniture or push toys

months 10–14
stands alone

months 12–14
walks on her own

months 14+
walks well; can pull toys

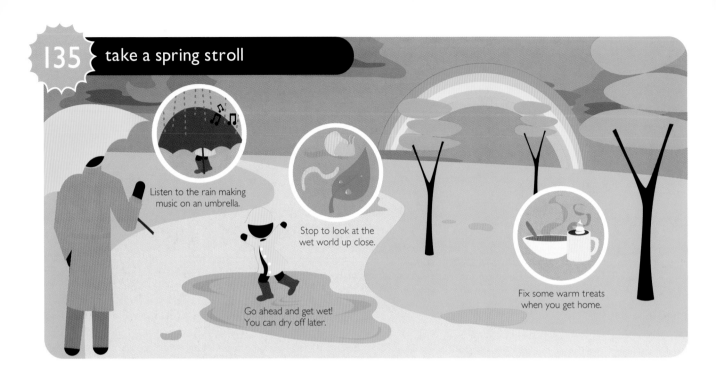

135 take a spring stroll

Listen to the rain making music on an umbrella.

Stop to look at the wet world up close.

Go ahead and get wet! You can dry off later.

Fix some warm treats when you get home.

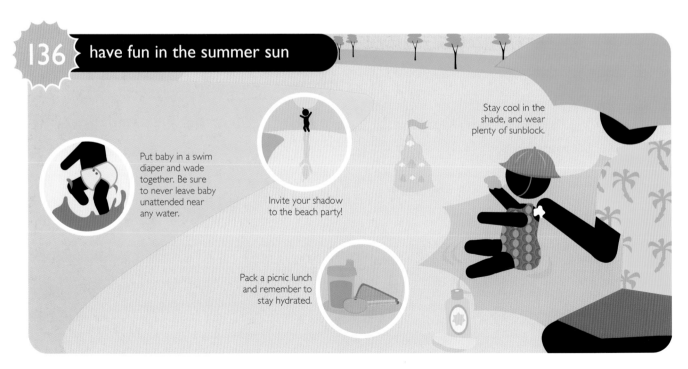

136 have fun in the summer sun

Put baby in a swim diaper and wade together. Be sure to never leave baby unattended near any water.

Invite your shadow to the beach party!

Pack a picnic lunch and remember to stay hydrated.

Stay cool in the shade, and wear plenty of sunblock.

Catch falling leaves together.

Collect treasures as you explore.

Sink into a leaf bed and watch the autumn sky.

Crunch leaves and kick up a shower.

Catch snowflakes.

Make tracks and snow angels.

Build snow bricks in plastic kitchen containers.

Take baby on a sled ride through the snow.

Mix eggs with food coloring.

Add greens; scramble.

Cook thoroughly.

Serve with chopped ham.

Arrange finger foods.

Strap baby in.

Add animal crackers.

Go on safari.

Spread sauce on pitas.

Sprinkle on cheese.

remove stubborn stains 90

Get silly with toppings.

Bake, slice, and serve.

1 c (240 ml) juice
2 packets gelatin

Mix juice and gelatin.

1 c (240 ml) juice

Heat additional juice.

Combine juices.

Stir until gelatin dissolves.

Pour into ungreased pan.

3 hr

Refrigerate until set.

Cut and remove shapes.

Eat and enjoy.

Pour dirt into a bucket.

Add water; stir.

Pour into tin; dry in the sun.

Garnish with flowers.

144 > build a sand castle

Create a level area.

Dig up some extra sand.

Stack and shape with water.

Decorate and build a moat.

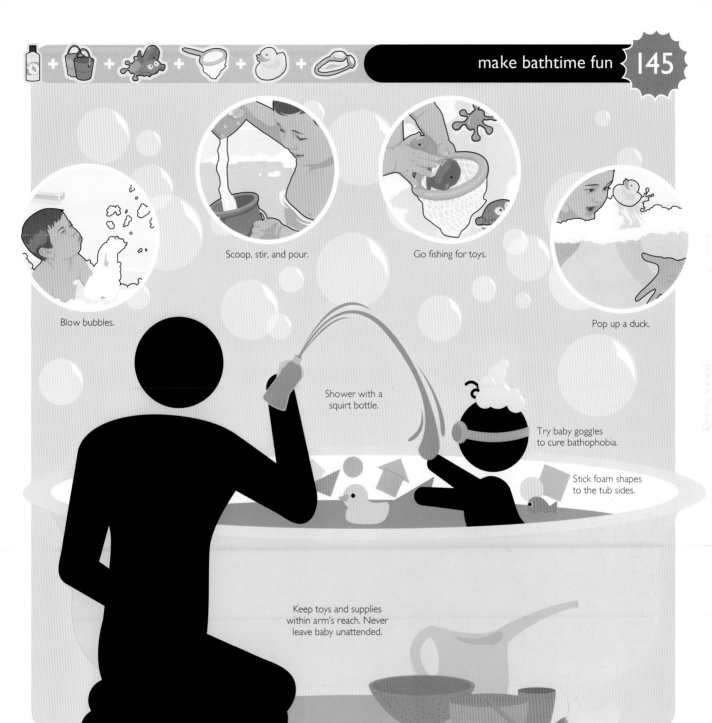

Blow bubbles.

Scoop, stir, and pour.

Go fishing for toys.

Pop up a duck.

Shower with a squirt bottle.

Try baby goggles to cure bathophobia.

Stick foam shapes to the tub sides.

Keep toys and supplies within arm's reach. Never leave baby unattended.

146 paint in the snow

Mix food color with water.

Pour into spray bottle.

Spray the snow.

Brrring on the fun!

147 paint with baby food

Gather the "paints."

Prepare to get messy.

Strap baby into high chair.

86 bathe a baby

Show baby how to paint.

Stimulate visual tracking.

Improve depth perception.

Encourage movement.

Let her take over.

Tape craft sticks together.

Use nontoxic markers.

Remove tape; mix up.

Put the puzzle together.

1 Seal box.

2 Cut seat and doors.

3 Score and fold windshield.

4 Cut out windsheld; tape.

5 Glue on plate wheels.

6 Attach cup lights.

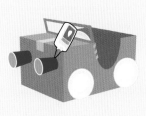

7 Get a custom paint job.

8 Add upholstery.

* Don't hog all the fun for yourself. When it's time to paint, let baby help customize his new ride.

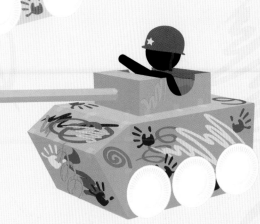

1 Cut and fold the paper.

2 Sew the pages together.

3 Cut the cardboard.

4 Space cardboard on cloth.

152   read a book together

Pick sturdy books.

Look at photos of faces.

Get animated!

Describe the pictures.

5 Trim the cloth.

6 Glue cardboard to cloth.

7 Fold and glue corners.

8 Glue back and front pages.

Reread baby's favorites.

Limit outside distractions.

Personalize the stories.

Use sound effects.

 If baby is enjoying a story, read it again. You might get bored, but babies love repetition.

Choose a setting.

Make baby the hero.

State the objective.

Introduce a villain.

Defeat the villain . . .

. . . in a nonviolent way.

Achieve the objective.

Live happily ever after.

Shadow puppets help make storytime fun and imaginative. Here are a few creatures to start with, but the possibilities are endless.

gorilla

wolf

moose

ox

bat

panther

parrot

antelope

swan

A time capsule is a fun way to collect and archive memories from baby's first years. (Plus: burying memories in your yard means more storage space in your closet!) When he's old enough, discovering the time capsule will be a great adventure. So make sure to store everything in an airtight container—and don't lose the map!

baby's original art

family tree

newspaper from the day baby was born

souvenirs

family photo album

sonograms

recording of baby's voice

draw a treasure map 156

Sketch the backyard.

Measure in paces . . .

. . . or by GPS marker.

Secure the map.

tools

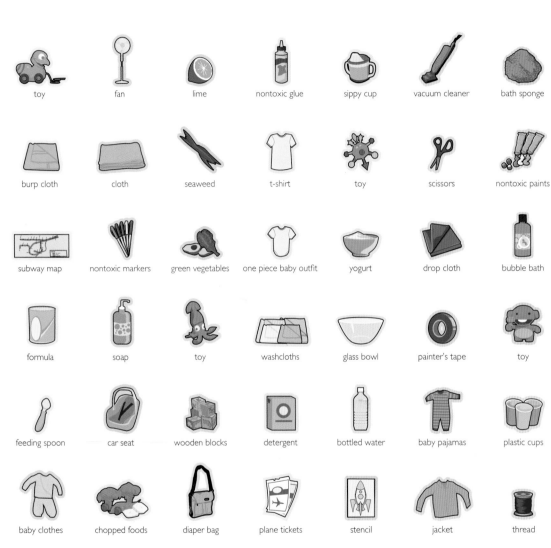

toy	fan	lime	nontoxic glue
sippy cup	vacuum cleaner	bath sponge	toy
burp cloth	cloth	seaweed	t-shirt
toy	scissors	nontoxic paints	sliced vegetables
subway map	nontoxic markers	green vegetables	one piece baby outfit
yogurt	drop cloth	bubble bath	small bites of food
formula	soap	toy	washcloths
glass bowl	painter's tape	toy	wall paint
feeding spoon	car seat	wooden blocks	detergent
bottled water	baby pajamas	plastic cups	pizza box
baby clothes	chopped foods	diaper bag	plane tickets
stencil	jacket	thread	toys
high chair	toy	personal lubricant	baby wipes
bib	iron	tomato sauce	theatre tickets

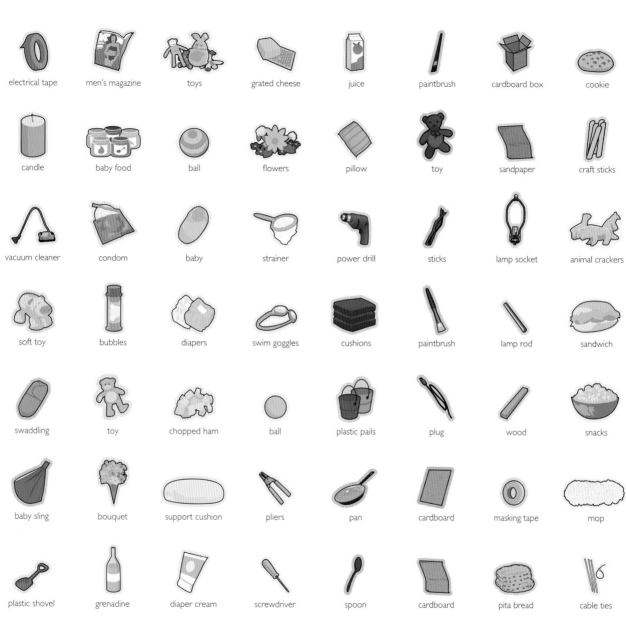

electrical tape	men's magazine	toys	grated cheese	juice	paintbrush	cardboard box	cookie
candle	baby food	ball	flowers	pillow	toy	sandpaper	craft sticks
vacuum cleaner	condom	baby	strainer	power drill	sticks	lamp socket	animal crackers
soft toy	bubbles	diapers	swim goggles	cushions	paintbrush	lamp rod	sandwich
swaddling	toy	chopped ham	ball	plastic pails	plug	wood	snacks
baby sling	bouquet	support cushion	pliers	pan	cardboard	masking tape	mop
plastic shovel	grenadine	diaper cream	screwdriver	spoon	cardboard	pita bread	cable ties
barbershop quartet	nail file	picnic basket	matches	dirt	spatula	plain gelatin	towel

nontoxic crayons

 baby shampoo

 paper plates

 spray bottles

 drink strainer

 home stereo

 weights

 ninja costumes

 rubber duck

 paper

 eggs

 baby bathtub

 cookie cutters

 pins

 staple gun

 fine paintbrush

 pencil

 collar and cuffs

 breast milk bag

 drill bit

 portable stereo

 nail clipper

 earphones

 box cutter

 lemonade

 nontoxic glue

 resealable bag

 gaming system

 drinking glass

 string

 flashlight

 high-contrast art

 toy

 black marker

 snacks

 pie tin

 measuring spoon

 whisk

 cell phone

 wire hangers

 pillow

 bottle

 iron-on paper

 pliers

 saucepan

 GPS system

 pan

 smartphone

 book pages

 paper towels

 ice

 spoon

 paint tray

 safe

 ruler

mirror

 shells

 hand mirror

 martini glass

 tape

 pot with lid

 nontoxic food color

stroller bag

color printer

index

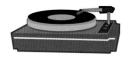

132

125

140

11

66

show me who

weldonowen

415 Jackson Street
San Francisco CA 94111
www.wopublishing.com

CEO, President Terry Newell

VP, Sales and
New Business Development Amy Kaneko

VP, Publisher Roger Shaw

Creative Director Kelly Booth

Executive Editor Elizabeth Dougherty

Project Editor Jann Jones

Assistant Editor Katharine Moore

Designers Rachel Liang, Meghan Hildebrand

Illustration Coordinator Conor Buckley

Production Director Chris Hemesath

Production Manager Michelle Duggan

Production Coordinator Charles Mathews

Color Manager Teri Bell

parenting
magazine

2 Park Avenue
New York NY 10016
www.parenting.com/store

Editorial Director Ana Connery

Executive Editors Shawn Bean and
Elizabeth Anne Shaw

Parenting and Weldon Owen are divisions of
BONNIER

Library of Congress Control Number: 2010941203
ISBN: 978-1-61628-111-3

10 9 8 7 6 5 4 3 2 1
2014 2013 2012 2011

Printed in China by 1010

Special thanks to:

Storyboarders
Sarah Duncan, Sheila Masson, Jamie Spinello,
Brandi Valenza, Astrea White, Kevin Yuen

Illustration specialists
Hayden Foell, Jamie Spinello, Ross Sublett

Editorial and research support team
Kendra DeMoura, Emelie Griffin, Marianna
Monaco, Gail Nelson-Bonebrake, David Sackrider,
Marisa Solís

Extra thanks to Mariah Bear and Lucie Parker for
their Show Me expertise.

A **Show Me Now** Book.
Show Me Now is a trademark
of Weldon Owen Inc.
www.showmenow.com

ILLUSTRATION CREDITS

The artwork in this book
was a true team effort. We are happy to thank and
acknowledge our illustrators.

Front Cover: **Tina Cash Walsh:** toy, pacifier **Britt Hanson:**
info people, stroller **Paula Rogers:** changing diaper

Back Cover: **Juan Calle (Liberum Donum):** impregnate
Steve Balesta: mix formula **Gabhor Utomo:** make baby
laugh

Key bg=background, fr=frames

Steve Baletsa: 21, 59–60, 70, 77–78 **Conor Buckley:** 12
bg, 17, 24, 35–37, 70 bg, 112 bg, 119 bg, 140 bg, 143 bg,
151 **Juan Calle (Liberum Donum):** 1–5, 11, 16, 18, 20 fr,
23, 30–32, 43–44, 49–51, 65–68, 71–73, 94–97 fr,
108–111, 112–113 fr, 125–126, 131–133, 153, 155–156
Tina Cash–Walsh: 76, 79, 82, 85–88 **Hayden Foell:** 13,
22 **Britt Hanson:** 19, 41, 62, 83, 90, 114, 135–138, 145
bg **Vick Kulihin:** 27, 29, 34, 38, 40 **Raymond Larrett:** 69
Rachel Liang: 6, 45 **Christine Meighan:** 99, 139, 141,
143 **Paula Rogers:** 7, 12, 61, 63–64, 74–75, 80, 84, 120,
146, 148 **Ross Sublett:** 15 **Bryon Thompson:** 10 bg, 14,
20 bg, 81–82, 94–97 bg, 121–124, 150 **Lauren Towner:**
105, 115–116, 119, 134 **Gabhor Utomo:** 8–9, 10 fr, 26,
39, 46–48, 53–58, 84, 89, 93, 98, 101–104, 106–107,
117–118, 127–130, 140, 142, 144, 145 fr, 147, 149, 152
Mary Zins 25, 28, 33, 91, 100, 154